Elasticated Waistbands

New Poems

By
Catherine Scott

Other poetry books by Catherine Scott

A Woman with a View. 2013
Add verse to Therapy. 2015
The Brazen Maiden from Hull. 2017
A Woman with a Grudge. 2019
Empty Busses. 2021

ISBN 978-0683455-0-0

Edition 2025

Published by Muse Publishing, 1, Soutergate, Barton upon Humber, DN18 6HG

Designed by Reflex Graphic Design 01225 832551

Photograph of Catherine Scott by kind permission of ??

Preface

Welcome to my sixth poetry collection. As with my other books, this one too has taken two years to put together but I'm equally excited by it. I never thought I'd get this far!

There are, of course, favourite poems from my other collections or performances that many have enjoyed. Rest assured, these will never leave my side at Spoken Word events and the collections in which they appear will remain available for as long as their print run lasts out.

A big thank-you to my family and friends for their on-going support and encouragement. I particularly express my gratitude to Lou Duffy-Howard who read my manuscript and was kind enough to add her endorsement as expressed on the back page of this book. Her own insightful seminal online celebration of River Hull and its environment is widely respected, so I particularly value her words.

I would also acknowledge the careful work of Muse Publishing which has supported me and appreciated my style and purpose. I greatly appreciated the work of Richard Ireland of Rexgraphic ,whose sensitive design skills have developed our ideas with inspiration.

There are also those, too numerous to mention, some who have specifically and others unwittingly, contributed to my material and I deeply appreciate their help and inspiration.

Finally. I also thank you those of you who had read my previous work and been brave enough to come back for more.

I really hope you enjoy this book as much as I did to write it.

Poems

Fun

Crumbs

Elasticated Waistbands

Having A Clear Out

Kit Kat Dilemma

The Look

Mansome

Softy Pofty

Pigs in Muck

This'll See Us Out

They Must Have Come
Into Money

Other Stuff

Body Clock

One Shot

Flash

What Might My Mother Say?

Supermarket Shopping

Over-Cooked

Persist

Tiddly Dum

You Can't Go Wrong

Friday Night Drama

Shackled

Moon Time

Moon Mad Millionaires

Little Things

The Dress

Once A Year

It's A Con

People

All Round Good Egg

It hasn't happened often in my life
But from time to time I've come across a guy I instinctively like
A David type of guy

He's not a slap you on the back, 'call me Dave' type of guy
Not an over the top, 'Anyone for tennis?' type of guy
Not a flamboyant, outrageous or extreme type of guy

But more of a poetic, quiet, a sort of get things done, type of a guy
An understanding, 'I know what you mean,'
A 'leave it to me, I'll do my best to sort it,' type of a guy

A guy who listens
A guy with vision
Who stays with the issue
Of what's relevant to you

To sum it up, he's just a rather nice guy
A decent, caring, gentle guy
A David

There should be more like him in the world

He's someone frankly, I'm proud to know
Someone who everyone who knows him knows
Is honest and genuine and as the old saying goes
You get what you see and you see what you get
He's a proper, hard-working all-round good egg.

A Million Dollars in Waitrose

Can someone possibly explain to me
Why it is I can guarantee
When I go out in my scruff I'm sure to see
An old school friend who looks better than me?

Today it was Hilary who somehow effortlessly has
That certain million-dollar class
But I know Hilary is not up to scratch
I heard she's had Botox on her ass

In an effort to avoid, I look the other way
But she has spotted me and she's heading my way
'Ewww hello, Dahhhrling…nice to see
Didn't think Waitrose was your cup of tea'

I'd tolerated her cruelty when we were at school
But revenge is a dish best served cool
'Why Hilary helloooo, gosh, you've not changed a bit
That face lift has helped, and you're still a bitch.'

An Item

Edna and Steve. Steve and Edna.
No-one knew who came first and did it really matter?
Always together. Always the same
The world was safe.

Enjoyed the same interests
Supported the same team
Argued, made up
An item

A strong, sound couple

Steve joined a gym
To shed a few pounds
'For you,' he told Edna

Edna joined the u3a
For herself

A few cracks appeared
In the lives of the safe, sound couple

New neighbours arrived
Awful kids
Telly on loud
Rows every night

Reassured Edna and Steve breathed a sigh of relief
They were O.K.
Weren't they?
Or at the very least they weren't nearly as bad as that

Edna and Steve, Steve and Edna
Did what most couples do
They papered over the cracks and stuck together

They each had flings
Fun, painful experiences
Understood by the other but never discussed
Life was sad, real, exciting and promiscuous

And in their 80's the safe, sound couple
Are still together
Still happy, still safe, still sound,

'Joined at the hip,' people said

But beneath the veneer
Edna and Steve, Steve and Edna
Secretly question if it could have been better
Had they only been brave enough
To join up with the delicious Julie or the sexily creative Frank?

Politics

Apathy

I can sense it in the air
In the way we breathe
In the way we walk

Apathy…
And it's dangerous

There is no energy
No fight
No umph

People are weary of the news
So they avoid it

The wars
The fraud
The lies

It's all too much
So they watch something mindless instead

The truth is too stressful
Too difficult
If they don't watch it, it's not happening

People feel powerless
And they have disengaged

They feel drained
Exhausted
And sick to the back teeth

They don't know which way to turn
Or who to trust

People are thinking they need to put themselves first
Because if they don't
Nobody else will

And I don't know what it's going to take
To change that

But to end on a high note
At least we don't live in America
Because that place is a disaster waiting to happen

Afghanistan

August 2021

Heart breaking Afghanistan
Taken over by the Taliba Ban
Brave men fighting in the name of Islam

It's easy to be brave with a gun in your hands
Against unarmed civilians

Religion anyone?
No thanks

Bouncing Back

In May 2020 in an attempt to get the economy back on track Rishi Sunak (the then Chancellor) introduced The Bounce Back Loan Scheme. It was intended to help businesses after Lock down ...but

Oh My Gawd
The system's flawed
4.9 billion lost to fraud
And I'd bet a penny to a pound that most of it's abroad

This governments naivety
Bordered on stupidity
Rubber stamping Bounce Back Loans for zero productivity

The criminals had a field day. they couldn't believe their luck
'It's money for old rope,' they cried and laughed like pigs in muck
'£50,000 lads, get it while you can
The country's in a pickle and Sunak* is our man'

'You just create a bogus business, it doesn't matter what it's for
No-one's going to check you out they're not counting anymore
We're the crafty schemers
Who can take them to the cleaners

And the fraudsters danced and gambled
Sang, 'This government's a shambles,
If we follow their example
We'll get more than ample
They're busy lining their pockets so we should do the same
Because you can bet your life a chance like this won't come our way again'

And it was who you knew
Not what you knew
When it came to the lucrative contracts
For there's always someone at the top ready to take advantage

And the low life scammers of this world couldn't give a monkey's toss,
About the poor, the sick and helpless or the people less well off
Covid didn't worry them, it was just an opportunity
To screw the system, make some dough then abandon their community

Their greed and selfishness
Has cost us
And Rishi Sunak
Thought they'd pay it back!
Those scammers are smarter than you mate

The man on The Clapham Omnibus is smarter than you mate
It's gone mate…
That 4.9 billion has fucking gone mate
To that great fucking fuck-over in the sky mate

Time to face the facts Sunak
Time to face the facts
And damned well get that money back

'Cos you were the chancellor back then
And now you've been promoted to P.M.
Now that's what I call bouncing back

*Rishi Sunak lead the Conservatives into a General Election in July
2024 and lost by a landslide. He resigned. As I write there are 6
contenders vying for the job.*

It's Party Time

(May 2022)

My name is Boris Johnson – I can do whate're I like
I'm going to hold a party – now who should I invite?
They need to be discreet and keep their dicks tucked in their pants
It shouldn't be a problem – I know lots of sycophants

I must be very careful - it needs to go without a hitch
But there's no need to worry 'cos - no-one likes a snitch
If we're caught I'll simply lie and say I didn't have a clue
I thought it was a working lunch for myself and all my crew

They need to let their hair down, they need a pint or two
A sausage roll and pizza are more than overdue
The public understands that we sometimes flaunt the rules
It doesn't matter that we made them – I mean – it's hardly headline news

Now the press have had their field day, they've had fun with Partygate
And I'm sure the people understand I've got a lot upon my plate
There's no way I'm resigning, I've made that clear enough
I'm not going anywhere, I'm intent on staying put

And I'm sorry, yes, I'm sorry for the folks who've had it tough
Who have lost their jobs and loved ones and as if that weren't enough
Every household bill is rising, they're going up and up
But I've promised them a rebate – now that should shut them up

Yes, my strategy is crafty, my diversion plan elite
With a little bit of bribery from the master of deceit
I can fool them into thinking I am meeting all their needs
And this problem will blow over in just a few short weeks

When everything has quietened down and the next election's due
I'll organise a reshuffle that is sure to see me through
For there is no doubt about it I am bound to stay in post
For the Faithful Tories recognise I'm a first-class party host

*In September 2022 Boris Johnson was replaced by Liz Truss as P.M.
She lasted 40 days to be replaced by Rishi Sunak until the General
Election in 2024 in which the Tories lost to Labour in a landslide
victory.*

Covid Rich

After Covid my husband and I were shopping in a furniture shop. The assistant told us that after the lockdowns they had never had so much cash through their tills before. People had been doing 'guvvies'(local term for cash in hand jobs) during Covid whilst at the same time taking furlough. Now the Covid crisis was over they were keen to spend their cash on high-end goods which they couldn't previously afford. I believe the same thing happened with holiday companies who sold more luxury end holidays than they had in years.

This is where the term 'Covid Rich' originated.

Cor! We're Covid Rich
That what we is
We took the furlough
And did guvvies as well
Cor! We're Covid Rich

We were in demand
Got cash in hand
No questions asked
We wore our masks
And tweaked the rules, like those in command

So now we're Covid Rich
Cor! We're Covid Rich
We've accrued a stash
Of Covid cash
We just have to decide how to spend it

I suppose now we can afford it we might even choose
To get ourselves pierced or weirdly tattooed
We might buy a Ferrari
We might book a Safari
We might treat ourselves to a five-star cruise

We'll acquire premier tickets for The Leicester Square Flicks
We'll go shopping in Harrods and Harvey Nicks
We'll pay Tiffanys a visit
Their jewellery's exquisite
The world is our oyster now we've got a few quid

14

We could go to Cheltenham, hire a box
There's exclusive hospitality for those in posh frocks
We could dine at The Ritz
Amidst the glamour and glitz
You'd be shocked what this money's unlocked

Covid provided a unique opportunity
To make lots and lots of illegal money
We fiddled the books
But, you know, needs must…
And at the time we thought it was funny

But now our exploits have come back to haunt us
The HMRC are on to us
They're on our backs
For unpaid tax
I fear they'll make an example of us

Well, I'm sorry, Your Honour, but it was fun while it lasted
We took our chance while the toffs got plastered
We made a mint
But now we're skint
And it seems we're about to get shafted

But pandemics only happen every now and again
So you can rest assured we'll never do it again
And I'm wondering if
For the sake of the kids
You could let us off with a slap on the wrist?

And to be honest, Your Honour, we just didn't think
For a few measly quid we'd end up in the clink
Can't we call it quits
'Cos my Mum's in bits
Say, 'Yes,' and I'll buy you a drink

'Yes please,' cried the judge, 'and make mine a double
'It's Friday afternoon and my head's in a muddle
'The system's fucked
'We're all corrupt
'Case dismissed for a kiss and a cuddle'

Vladimir Putin

(To be sung to the tune of the children's song 'I think I'll go and eat worms').

Nobody likes him
Everybody hates him
I wish he'd go and eat worms
His government is just a farce
I'd like to kick him up the arse
And watch him wriggle and squirm

His generals should show some guts
Some courage and a pair of nuts
But it seems that no one dares
They dance like puppets on a string
Whilst he plays with his ding-a-ling
All of them are scared

Oligarchs and hangers on
You won't survive an Atom bomb
You need to watch your step
Putin is a psychopath
Whose led you up the garden path
Whilst the West has overslept

It's getting worse by the hour
No one man should have that power
How could he sink so low?
We need to do away with him
Join the queue to kick him in
It's time for him to go

Heading downwards in a spin
What a state the world is in
I think we're all agreed
Failure's not an option here
Our intentions must be very clear
The Ukraine must succeed

Get your coat on Vladimir
Get the hell out of here
No more caviar
No more threats and no more bribes
No more of your filthy lies
You have gone too far

Vladimir Putin
Everybody hates him
At last the world has learned
He really is a piece of work
A nasty, rotten, little squirt
Who should be eaten by worms

Executive Lies

Re: The Post Office scandal 2022 – but has been on-going for a lot longer

It has taken over twenty years
Of heart ache and tears
Ruined lives
Suicides
And hundreds of blighted careers

Twenty four years
Of jibes and jeers
Executive lies
Sleepless nights
And reputations besmirched by smears

Enter sub postmaster Alan Bates
Who refused to admit he'd made mistakes
Who stood his ground
Who refused to back down
A thorn in the flesh to those snakes

Alan Bates is a man with a spine
Who fought for those victims accused of crime
He didn't call it a day
Or walk away
But selflessly gave of his time

Now Rishi and his ministers are on it
Well, it is election year innit?
They want it all sorted
And the victims supported
Did I hear someone say I'm a cynic?

Twenty four years on and there's a public enquiry
Might I suggest you make a note in your diary
It'll make interesting listening
They'll be jostling and jiggling
And they'll all blame each other entirely

The People at The Top

Another poem about the Post Office Scandal

Somebody at the top knows who dunnit
Somebody at the very top knows who dunnit
Who's responsible for the cover up
Because without a doubt there's been a cover up
And there's one thing certain:
They're all in it together

But the people at the top
The people at the very top
Have got each other's back
And so far, no-one, has had the decency to blow the gaff
No doubt too busy saving their own necks
Frightened of losing their pension cheques

Instead, the people at the top
The people at the very top
Preferred
To declare
That their long-standing, honest, hard-working, sub-postmasters
Were fraudsters,
No better than common criminals
When they were, in fact, the victims
Of the massively over-priced, incapable of doing the job, Horizon
computer system
Which the people at the top
The people at the very top
Commissioned
And for years and years refused to admit
That there was a glitch
Too cowardly to admit they'd made a mistake
But someone surely has to pay?

It is a scandal,
A national scandal
It's nothing short of corruption
About a system that didn't function

It's an outrage
An absolute outrage
That the cowards at the top
Those cowards at the very top
Broke those honest, hard-working men and women
Some of whom were sent to prison

There's an investigation now
The public cannot understand how
How the people at the top
The people at the very top
Have so far got away with it

But somebody knows who dunnit
Some shameless low life knows who dunnit
They must be getting well paid for it
Keeping their traps shut
Whilst taking their cut

I want to know who dunnit
I want to know who dunnit
I want them sent to prison for it
For a long time
For a bloody long time

God only knows
How they can live with themselves
Because I know I couldn't

Climate Change

In 2016 or thereabouts the computer system of Climate Change – or Crew was hacked. No one has ever discovered who the hackers were but they managed to delay the work to change the direction of the climate change program by a devastating 10 years. We now only have 10 years in which to put the world to rights rather than the 20 we would have originally had. King Charles has been telling us about climate change for 40 years and no-one has taken any notice. You would think that being who he is that he would be in a position to influence powerful people.

Fake News

Trump laughs in the face of the scientific findings
And confidently announces
'Don't listen to them. It's Fake News
It's all Fake News.'

He scoffs and puffs out his chest, 'Those scientists must be deranged
There's no such thing as climate change'
I am a very stable genius
And I know these things

Trump v Harris
(Early November 2024)

'It's too close to call,' they're sayin',
But my gut tells me that he'll get in

And behind the walls of the Kremlin
Putin is laughin'
'Look, Comrades, this is democracy in Action.'

I despair
For America

*Trump won by a significant majority

Global Nightmare

Donald Trump has won – again
He says he'll make America great again
But the people forgot to ask, 'Who for?'

I especially can't understand why women
Would vote for him?
They have surely let their standards slip
For God's sake ladies get a grip
And protect your daughters
From those marauders

Donald won't be listening to his advisors
He'll drag America into a crisis
Whilst constantly claiming to be the wisest
President they've ever electsizest

But outsiders see
A catastrophe
They see
The American Dream
Becoming a Global Nightmare

And Putin
In the Kremlin
Smiles

He'll Make America Great Again

(November 2024)

The world became a more dangerous place
When Donald Trump won The White House race
A convicted felon, a misogynist
Savagely pursuing his politics
But you'll be alright
So long as you're white

Climate change will be fake news a gain
There's a reasonable chance he'll dismiss The Ukraine
Will he pull out of NATO?
We just don't know
But he'll Make America Great Again

Regardless of their qualification
He'll appoint his cronies above their station
And they, of course, will be just fine
Whilst they lick his boots and toe the line   '

Donald will sort out all the immigrants
The sick, the poor and the innocents
He'll end inflation
He'll restore the nation
And Make America Great Again.

He's decided he'll be imposing tariffs
Though he's yet to learn what a tariff is
But I'm sure the Chinese will set him straight
When they passively, aggressively retaliate

A fucking nincompoop
Is on the loose
But you'll be alright so long as you're wealthy
Able-bodied, fit and healthy

Oh yeah! He'll Make America Great Again

Vladimir Putin must be laughing his socks off
He can't believe his tactics have paid off
'Thank you, thank you Donald Trump
'All my birthdays have come at once.'

The fact this has happened in America
Is proof it can happen anywhere
And I despair
For America

Think of the Kids

'Eat out to Help out,' laughed Sunak
Before he packed his bags
He's gone
Bloody good

Boris Johnson promised an extra £365 million per week for the NHS
If we'd just vote 'OUT'
And unbelievably people believed him
He's on his Boris bike
Not before time
Bloody good

In forty days Liz Truss
Had the economy stuffed
And now she's lost her seat
Well, bloody good

The people voted Labour
Because they were sick of the Tory lies
The lies and lies and lies and lies
Their bloody lies

And rather than vote Labour
Some Tories voted for that Fart Arse
Farage
Bloody hell

I'm sorry to say I'm losing hope
And with Trump in the White House it's a slippery slope
God only knows where this will end
The worry of it drives me round the bend

Please don't tell me it's going to be alright
Because it's not going to be alright
Think of the kids
Think of the kids
For pity's sake think of the kids

Oh bloody hell
Oh bloody hell
Oh, bloody, bloody hell

How Dare You?

I found a message in a plastic bottle
Floating on the sea
It said, 'You are ruining our lovely world
You are sabotaging our lovely world
How dare you?'

It felt personal

It went on: Climate change
War
Greed
You ruining our beautiful world
How dare you?

Sorry to be the bearer of bad news but
Stop saying, 'We've still got time'
Because we haven't
It's run out
You are ruining our amazing world
How dare you?

Species extinct
Floods
Famine
Heat
And worst of all Greed
And maniacal lust for power
Stop ruining our fantastic world
How dare you?'

People think it won't happen
But it will.
Stop.
Think.
About the future
About the **children**

Where's the Compassion?
The Common Sense?
The Fundamental Understanding?
The **Love**

Might as well face it
We're up the spout
It's gone
Thanks so much to the spineless politicians

27

Hypocrisy

Oh! America what have you done?
What a sad, sad nation you've become
A land where it's legal to carry a gun
And refuse a woman an abortion

I'm wondering which planet you're coming from?

And the self-righteous, Pro-Lifers cheer
'This is the pinnacle of my career
No more will babies be aborted
My faith in God has been rewarded'

So prejudiced, so blinkered, so narrow minded
They declare without a shred of kindness
'My dear, you know this is 'God's Will'
There can be no morning-after pill'

Appointed by Trump, The Supreme Court Judges
Have failed to grasp how serious this is
Have failed to acknowledge the desperation
They have failed the women of their nation

Yet look who's thriving, why it's the NRA
And the right-wing, do-gooders turn away
It seems they've neither the courage or will
To challenge the Big Boys on Capitol Hill

I despair of their hypocrisy
I fear for their democracy

So, children in schools need increased protection
From gun carrying psychopaths with deadly intention
And abused, pregnant women are broken and shackled
And easy prey victims of a system double-barrelled

So watch your back
Because the next minority group to be under attack
Could be yours
And rest assured
No-one will be listening

In America, compassion
Has gone out of fashion

Greed Disease

I'm sorry to say it but the sad fact is
We've had the good times
They're over
Done and dusted
Gone

Buried under years of consecutive governments
Who refuse to believe
Admit
Or act upon
The evidence

Climate change
Greed
Disease
It's there for all to see
You don't need to be a genius to work it out

Not one government throughout the whole world
Is brave enough to stand alone
To stand out
And speak the truth
About our children's future

I'm terrified
And furious
There's no leadership
Everyone's busy saving their own necks
Their own wealth

We're living in a sick, sick
World
And we're losing our planet
Our beautiful, amazing planet
To greed

And please, PLEASE
Do not tell me
To pray

Knacked Off

We're short of experienced public sector workers
Policemen, teachers, doctors, nurses,
Highly-skilled professionals
Frustrated individuals
Have left their jobs
And knacked off

They took a glance
And took a stance
And knacked off

They waved goodbye to all that tension
Deciding instead withdraw their pension
And who can blame 'em?

Now The Tories have panicked and asked
If they, 'Could possibly go back?'
They're having a laugh

'You what??'
They scoffed
'We're the-newly-retired-over-fifty-fives
'And we are having the time of our lives!
'Go back to that!
'All that graft?
'Unappreciated and understaffed
'Do you think we're bloody daft?'

'Rejoin the Rat Race to save your skin?
'And help you lot to get back in?
'We don't think so
'No, we don't think so'

We can't begin to express
The level of stress
Caused by unempathic bosses breathing down our necks
Simply because you refused to invest

Now, you've caused the problem
So you sort it out
But frankly my dears, it's time you were out
So do us all a favour, pack your bags
And knack off

Because we, the over fifty-fives,
Are finally having,
The time of our lives

Broken

I wrote this poem after watching a shocking television documentary about the fate of British women who are being failed by the courts and escaping to Cyprus to escape violent, abusive former partners. There is no extradition treaty with Cyprus.

Along with hundreds of others
She fled with her child to Cyprus
After the English Family Courts decreed
That access to his father must be agreed

The father was a proven violent and aggressive man
A former prisoner and unreformed man
A horrible, nasty piece of work man
A man who was not a man

The judge accused her of alienation
And added that since their separation
She had turned their son against his father
And more over that he must see his father
At all costs
At any cost…
And ultimately at their cost

The Family Court
Ignored the police and hospital reports
They ignored the overwhelming proof
And categorically denied the truth
Of his repeated, unprovoked attacks
And made her felt like she was going mad

She went to court believing in the British Justice System
And she came out broken

The Courts failed them
But they cannot extradite them
From Cyprus

Health

Crocs

For Polly

The overweight man was there most mornings
Balding, sweating, stinking, boring
His shorts were red, and his shirt and his socks
But his footwear was trendy, he always wore crocs

Fat man annoyed us, he got on our nerves
Every day he would try it on with the girls
I steered myself clear of his cauliflower breath
One whiff of that and I'd choke to death

'Nice day today,' was his chat up line
The trainer rolled her eyes and I rolled mine
His outfit alone would put most girls off
Then in walked Tracey, and she too wore crocs

Tracey was buxom, tattooed and loud
And when their eyes met it was love at first sight
They had a shared interest in red shorts, shirts and socks
And their relationship blossomed when they kicked off their crocs

Cholesterol

When diagnosed with high cholesterol
I had to learn to be sensible
Four weeks later I thought the nurse would be pleased
When I told her I'd managed to give up the cheese
But she shook her head said, 'I don't think so
With your family history you've not long to go.
I suggest you go home and grit your teeth
There's no point in fighting what lies beneath'

I cried, 'Why you cheeky little so and so
How you've held down your job I just don't know
And after the effort I've made in giving up cheese
You've the nerve to tell me I'll soon be deceased
You should encourage me to help myself
And take responsibility for my own health.'

She replied, 'I'm sorry my dear but I've no time for chat
You've refused the statins so I'm afraid that's that.
The history proves you're on a loser
Check out the stats on your computer.'

Her attitude got me properly rattled
And I'm pleased to report she got both barrels
I yelled, 'Frankly, my dear your attitude stinks
I'll prove you wrong before long, methinks.'

And I redoubled my efforts with the butter and cheese
I learned to say, 'no' instead of, 'yes please'
I cut down on sugar, on chocolate and cake
I gave up chips and slowed down on steak
I'm got big into berries, I'm nuts about nuts
I simply love apples and pears and stuff
But just once a week
I enjoy a treat:
A buttered scone with cream and jam
Am I cheating? Yes I am!

To be honest I think I deserve a medal
For lowering my cholesterol level
And the nurse received her just desserts
When she had no choice but to eat her words

What's it About?

In the 1960's a drunken idiot drove his car
Across the road
And hospitalized my sister
For 8 months

Which in itself was bad enough
But
In those days patients were allowed to smoke in bed
And my sister, then a non-smoker, bought cigarettes
From the trolley they wheeled around the wards:
My sister started smoking in hospital

She also started writing
On her back and with her leg up in traction she wrote and smoked
Smoked and wrote
And completed her first book:
Diamond Cuts Diamond
The first of ten novels

She was interviewed by the local newspaper

Who knows what might have happened if there hadn't been an accident?
Would she have written?
Would she have smoked?
Would she have died of cancer prematurely?
Who knows?

Fifty years have passed and the rules have changed
Drink driving is now a serious offence
Seat belts are compulsory
And smoking is not allowed in hospitals

And it's not about The Nanny State
It's not about our human rights
It's not about freedom of choice

It's about being responsible
And caring
And kind

It's about all the Marys in the world

He's Ours

Our Grandson moved in with us recently
He's changed our lives significantly
Whereas we used to go out without a backwards glance
Now everything must be planned in advance

Logan, is slightly autistic
Which makes him very repetitive
And stubborn
Yes, he's stubborn and repetitive
Repetitive
And stubborn
But we love him
Because, well you know, he's ours

Logan is fussy about what he'll eat
He'll accept chicken nuggets but refuse roast beef
He loves fish fingers and chips and jelly
He'll also eat yoghurt (but not raspberry)

Without a shadow of a doubt
He's the master of the house
But that's O.K. because he's well, you know, he's ours

Life's funny sometimes, it catches you out
When you least expect it, it all turns about
We've had to adapt, it's been pretty rough
But you know the old saying, 'When the going gets tough?'
And we're not there yet, we've a way to go
But we're making headway, and well, y'know
We love him don't we…and he's ours

This poem is also in my book 'A Woman with a Grudge.'
I've included it in this book because it fits with other poems and
because it marks the start of a long journey of discovery regarding
my learning about autism.

Neuro Di-Verse

I wrote this in the midst of a struggle with the Education and Health Care Plan for my autistic grandson.

I feel like I'm drowning in a sea of paper work
I feel as though I'm sinking under the weight of the words
And even worse
I'm being urged
To agree to the words without reading them first

I can't decide, my head's in a whirl
About what I should do, about what to do first
And what is worse
I fear I might be losing it, I fear that I might burst
Administration is a bitch in the modern world

The authorities in power simply do not seem to care
That the system is unbalanced and the system is unfair
And even worse
They refuse to face the facts, they insist that they are right
Their arrogance and incompetence keep me awake at night

I wonder who can help me? How long will all this take?
It's difficult when you're fighting people who deny they make mistakes
And what is worse
Is that in the midst of all this nonsense, in the midst of this red tape
Is a little boy I love to bits who makes my old heart ache

He's unaware of the complexities, of the war going on behind him
He's unaware of the life he faces and the problems that surround him
And what is worse
He's not the first
And he won't be the last

Hurrah!
I've found someone who'll help me, a woman kind and caring
Who knows the ropes, understands his needs, who's brave and bold
and daring
And better still
She has the will
She's formidably determined

So stand clear all you Jobsworth
And mentally note this verse,
'We won't back down
It's your turn to drown
In the paperwork for the neuro diverse.'

Even Worse

I'm drowning in a sea of paper work
I'm suffocating in an ocean of words
And even worse
I'm being urged
To sign contracts without reading them first

I can't decide, my head's in a whirl
About what I should do, about what to do first
And what is worse
I think I'm going crackers, I'm scared that I might burst
Administration is a bitch in the modern world

The authorities in power simply do not seem to care
That the system is unbalanced and the system is unfair
And even worse
They refuse to face the facts, they insist that they are right
I'm sad to say their attitude keeps me awake at night

I wonder who can help me? How long will all this take?
It's difficult when you're fighting people who deny they make mistakes
And what is worse
Is that in the midst of all this nonsense in the midst of this red tape
Is a little boy who needs some help, who makes my old heart ache

He's unaware of the complexities, of the war going on behind him
He's unaware of the life he faces and the problems that surround him
And what is worse
He's not the first
And he won't be the last

Hurrah!
I've found someone who'll help me, a woman kind and caring
Who knows the ropes, understands his needs, who's brave
and bold and daring
And better still
She has the will
She's formidably determined

So stand clear all you Jobsworth
And mentally note this verse,
'We won't back down
It's your turn to drown
In the paperwork for the neuro diverse.'

40

It Shouldn't be Allowed

He could only have been in his twenties
Thin and unkempt
Hair long and bedraggled
Finger nails filthy and crackled
Worn out boots with broken laces
Trousers hanging for the want of braces

He was in the car park scrabbling in the dirt
And muttering to himself
Oblivious to the public and his surroundings
He was moving dirt and counting, counting

Mothers pulled their children away
Others, disgusted, looked the other way,
'This shouldn't be allowed
In the centre of town.'

A copper asked,
'You alright there, mate?'
The bloke didn't appear
To hear
He just carried on scrabbling
And babbling

Poor sod

The copper reached out, touched him, 'O.K. Mate?'
That was a mistake
Startled the bloke started shouting
**'LAND MINE, LAND MINE, LAND MINE
STAND BACK, GET BACK
STAND BACK, GET BACK
LAND MINE, LAND MINE, LAND MINE**

He scared the shit out of me

Roland had flashed back to Iraq
When his patrol had been attacked

BOOOOM!

It Takes Guts

It takes guts
To admit
You think you're going nuts
When everyone around you is apparently sane

You wonder, 'Is it just me?
Am I the only one who thinks like this?
Am I the only one who thinks the world is going mad
Or is it me?
Is it me that's mad?'

You conclude:
It's probably both

A Little Victory

I'm losing my words
And I'm feeling scared
Today, I couldn't remember the word for …I can't remember now
My brain somehow just wouldn't allow
Access to my mental dictionary
I don't have the vocabulary
I tell myself, 'It'll come back to me.'
And usually
Eventually
It does and for me that's a little victory
Everyday I have a little victory
Hurrah!

My husband's the same
We play a little game
We call it, 'Think of the word,'
It's a bit like 'I Spy' but without the words
But between us, usually
We come up with it…and that's our little victory
We celebrate each day with a victory

Now what was that word today? Oh yes…that's it…conservatory
We couldn't remember the word for 'conservatory.'
We looked at each other…sort of… confused
Then amused
Then puzzled
That's a good word…puzzled
Yes, I like that
I must remember that
'Puzzled'

This afternoon I'm playing a blinder
I suddenly remembered the word, 'ring-binder'
I don't know why but it just came to me
I didn't need it but it just came to me
Bill was impressed,
'Heck, Catherine,' he said, 'You'll be remembering who I am next!'

One of the hardest things is names
Family names
I go through the lot before I get to the right one
Michael, Ruth, Jenny, Rachel, Emma, Beth, Evie, Tom,
Tom, Tom…
Yes, that's the one
I knew I'd get there eventually…
Today's little victory

There's A Bridge Close By

I'm tight as a fucking bow string
I'm coiled as fucking spring
And when I'm asked to say what's wrong
I tell them, 'Everything'

'You need to be more specific
In order that we might help
Press one for drugs, two for abuse
And three for anything else'

I press three

A voice informs me: 'We understand where you're coming from
Please visit our web site: www.wedontgiveatoss.com'

There's a bridge close by

I don't visit their web site
I don't push any more buttons
It's pointless

I go to the bridge.

I feel calm
Resolved
Not at all how I expected to feel
But now, now, I've finally made up my mind
I feel O.K and strangely… safe
It feels easy
It's the right thing to do
I take in the view…
It's beautiful
And I'm warm and comfortable
Inside my self-made bubble

Well just look at that…ain't that just my luck?
Here comes the do-gooder
Running like fuck
He's waving at me to 'not give up'
I half wave back, 'I've had enough.'

He arrives, out of breath and terrified
More terrified
Than me
Actually
I make the mistake of looking in his eyes
And suddenly I'm terrified
Truly terrified

I look down:
It's a bloody long drop

He's panting, gasping for breath but he talks to me
Takes his time with me
And slowly
Very slowly
My resolve
Crumbles

I crumble

I fall to pieces

I'm terrified of living
I'm terrified of dying

What do I do?

He takes control
Holds me
I've not been held in a very long time

'It's O.K.' he says
'It'll be O.K.'
And I believe him.

Starting to Feel a bit Left Out

Lots of my friends have had one
And naturally, I'm pleased for them
But I'm starting to feel a bit …well, a bit left out

Sandra, Pat 1 and Pat 2, Sylvia, Denise, Janet and Alan
They've all had one
But not me
Not a sniff

I sing their praises
'You're doing amazing,
'You must be so pleased
'So relieved.'

They smile that they are, 'Truly delighted'
And, 'So impressed with the care provided
'The patience, the kindness, the expertise
'Has to be experienced to be believed.'

I admit I do feel jealous at the attention they're receiving
The level of praise is incongruent to the tasks that they're achieving
I'm shocked to see how easily they've taken to the limelight
I'm wondering if it's possible for me to get some limelight?
I want some limelight!

But their methodology
Puts the fear of God into me
There has to be another way
A less painful way
To get attention

Mmmmmmm

So, I've decided my claim to fame will be that I was never offered one
Because I never needed one
And people will comment that I'm truly amazing
Because I've never had a hip replacement

How times have changed

As a younger couple we were always surrounded by people
Mainly our kids
Needing attention
And time and money

Years ago, if we found ourselves unexpectantly on our own
We'd run upstairs giggling
And make the most of it
Enjoying a rare afternoon of sex and fun

Last week we found ourselves on our own
I looked across at Bill to see him fast asleep
Head back, mouth open,
The crossword awaiting his attention

I smiled a little ruefully
Thinking, 'How times have changed.'

Health and Safety

Health and Safety, Health and Safety
The world's gone mad on Health and Safety
I remember the time you could walk on site
Just do your job and go home at night
Nobody worried about Health and Safety

Now they're wanting kids to wear goggles for conkers
Are they having a laugh? They must be bonkers
But if your son or mine lost a tooth or an eye
We'd be the first in the queue to question, 'Why?'
And, 'Where were the Health and Safety?'

My Dad was a miner and I remember one night
He came home late and sat and cried
There'd been an accident and three men were dead
'There will have to be an inquiry,' he said
And they called for the Health and Safety

The triple trawler tragedy and Lil Bilocca
Who fought for the men who came a cropper
That disastrous fire at Grenfell Tower
People mourned and sent in flowers
Outraged about the Health and Safety

Funeral Plan

There it is
Done
My funeral plan
All prepared and ready
For My Big Day

I've named the Directors
'Cos I know they're good
I've looked into it you see
So I know they'll look after me
Properly

To save you the worry and expense
It's paid for in advance
'Cos I don't want any skimping

And don't be having me 'done'
I mean like, embalmed
I don't want that
But, I would like to have me toe nails painted
If you don't mind
I'd like to look nice

I'd like white flowers
I'll tell you to your face beforehand
If I decide otherwise
I'll let you know
So there you go
White flowers please – like my sister had

And, if it's all the same to you
I'd like a bit of a do
Few drinks, lots to eat
And someone good reciting me poetry

And Ruth singing
And everyone talking
And Mike – no crying
'Cos you're a lovely son and a special guy

50

And Bill – that's if you're still here
Don't go getting frisky with anyone else
And eat properly, and go out, and keep fit
And take care
And I'll see you again – or maybe not - depending on what's on
t'other side
If anything

But anyway, thanks for the ride
I reckon when push comes to shove and at the end of the day
We can pretty much say
That together we did it...we did O.K

Fun

Crumbs

They say it's a sign of madness to carry on doing the same thing
And still expect a different outcome
Nevertheless:-

I sweep
I wash
I clean down the sides
I dust
I vac

But no matter what
No matter how hard I try
Or how many times I clean
You can bet your life
At the end of the day
There will still be crumbs

I swear to God they wait
Craftily
Patiently
In every nook and cranny
They wait
Until the second I turn my back
Then out they jump

I can almost hear them laughing at me
'Look! Here she is again!
Got you again
Loser!'

There will always be crumbs

They stick two fingers up at me
They say, 'We've got you sussed
You'd best just accept it
You've no chance
You'll never win
Against us

Because we're The Crumbs
And we're here to stay.'

Elasticated Waistbands

I never thought this would happen to me but
I am…I'm rusting up
My joints need oiling
I'm at risk of falling
It seriously winds me up

I've noticed that my knees are creaking
And other parts have started squeaking
Where I used to be pert
Upright and alert
I now need considerable tweaking

And for reasons inexplicable
It seems I'm now invisible
There's little respect
For the age defect
An attitude I find despicable

My hearing is sharp, I can hold a conversation
I'm an absolute whizz at communication
But they talk over my head
To my daughter instead
We're the side-lined generation

That old age is a bitch it can't be denied
And I'm truly ecstatic to still be alive
I may be slower
But I'm still a go-er
I sport flaming red lippy with pride

I shun the elasticated waistbands
I ppfft at the greying hair strands
I don't need those
I want outrageous clothes
And to flirt wildly with young men in bands

The ageing process is slow and cruel
There's a steady decline in my friendship pool
But I retain my grip
And stiff upper lip
With the u3a as my finishing school

Having a Clear Out

It's Spring and I'm having a clear out
A proper clear out
A Spring Clean clear out

Everything's going
Old stuff
Broken stuff
Chipped stuff
Old papers I haven't looked at for years stuff
Stuff I haven't used for years stuff
Pretty much any old stuff

I don't need it
And it's going.

Nothing's safe
Including the kids
I think I'll probably throw myself in there too.

I'm taking a therapeutic trip
To the tip

That was yesterday
And couldn't you just guarantee that today
I need that cardigan

Kit Kat Dilemma

There's a Kit Kat in the fridge
There's a Kit Kat in the fridge
And it's talking to me
It's talking to me

It says, 'Open the door
'Open the door
And eat me
Eat me!

I tell myself I'm stronger than this
I'm stronger than the Kit Kat in the fridge
But it's hard to resist
The Kit Kat in the fridge

There are two Kit Kats in the fridge
Two Kit Kats in the fridge
A two finger Kit Kat
And a four finger Kit Kat

There are three Kit Kats in the fridge
Three Kit Kats in the fridge
A two finger Kit Kat
A four finger and a Chunky Kit Kat

There are four Kit Kats in the fridge
Four Kit Kats in the fridge
A two finger and a four finger Kit Kat
A Chunky and a Peanut Butter Kit Kat

There are five Kit Kats in the fridge
Five Kit Kats in the fridge
A two finger, a four finger, a Chunky Kit Kat
A Peanut Butter and a Caramel Kit Kat

There are six Kit Kats in the fridge
Six Kit Kats in the fridge
A two finger, a four finger, a Chunky Kit Kat
A Peanut Butter, a Caramel and a White Chocolate Kit Kat

There are seven Kit Kats in the fridge
Seven Kit Kats in the fridge
A two finger, a four finger, A Chunky, A Peanut Butter Kit Kat
A Caramel, a White Chocolate and a Dark Chocolate Kit Kat

There are eight Kit Kats in the fridge
Eight Kit Kats in the fridge
A two finger, a four finger, a Chunky, a Peanut Butter, a Caramel Kit Kat
A White Chocolate, a Dark Chocolate and an Orange Chocolate Kit Kat

There are nine Kit Kats in the fridge
Nine Kit Kats in the fridge
A two finger, a four finger, a Chunky, A Peanut Butter, a Caramel, a
White Chocolate Kit Kat
A Dark Chocolate, an Orange Chocolate and a Mint Chocolate Kit Kat

There are ten Kit Kats in the fridge
Ten Kit Kats in the fridge
A two finger, a four finger, a Chunky, A Peanut Butter, a Caramel,
a White Chocolate A Dark Chocolate Kit Kat
An Orange Chocolate, a Mint Chocolate and a bag of Kit Kat Bites

It was the Bites that dunnit Miss
The Bites that dunnit
And I'm ashamed to admit
That I ate every single one of those Kit Kats in the fridge

The Look

Fashion is not my bag, so to speak
There's some weird stuff out there on the street
Frankly, I think they're out of ideas

It seems to me
They put together the most awful colours
With the most awful styles
And tell us, 'It's 'The Look!'

Well, it's 'A Look' O.K., but it's not for me
Long dresses with bows and frills don't do it for me
I mean to say, 'Come on.
COME ON!!
Bows and frills?
BOWS AND FRILLS!!
For grown-ups?
They're having a laugh.

Come to think of it I didn't even like them as a child

And now the fashion gurus have teamed up the bows and frills
With heavy, black, thick souled, boots
Awful colours, awful styles, bows and fills, with boots
Lovely!
Ummmm!
Comfy!
Ummmm!

Next step
They throw on an ill-fitting cardigan
Which to my mind hangs uncomfortably off the shoulders
Of the model
But who nevertheless manages to pull off 'The Look'

The bitch

Frankly, she could wear a bin bag and still look amazing

Ummmm!
I could look like that if I bought that dress

I order the dress
And the boots
And the cardi

They arrived today and I look like shit

Mansome

It had been a long time, a very long time since we boarded
a plane for Spain
When Corona struck we had seriously thought we'd never
go there again
But the flight was perfect, the landing smooth, the transfer
a piece of cake
We settled ourselves in for a wonderful time and a long over-due
summer break

The first night we were exhausted, we fell headlong into bed
Then a woofer started woofing, he never paused for fucking breath
Woof! Woof! Yap! Yap! I wished that woofer dead
Yet my husband never heard him, he must be fucking deaf

The breakfast bar was chaos, the staff run off their feet
And greedy fuckers stuffed themselves with croissants, cake and meat
They wolfed down strings of sausages, they gobbled pancakes,
cheese and toast,
Then formed an orderly queue to await the evening roast

We thought we'd give the pool a go, the water looked inviting
But a couple still hung over started arguing and fighting
We had a laugh when she pushed him in, fully clothed
it served him right
Everything was kicking off at the Grand Hotel tonight

Opposite our balcony loomed a massive building site
As ever optimistic I checked the builders out
One smiled as he approached me, tall and dark and handsome
My legs went all a-quiver for that hunk of Spanish Mansome

We went to a Flamenco show, the dancers were fantastic
Castanets a-clacking, the atmosphere dramatic
One very brave male dancer wore a long flamenco dress
He swished his skirts seductively and gave Bill his home address

Before embarking at the airport we thought we'd have a little snack
But when I saw the price of it I put the Kit Kat back
Outraged I cried, 'What a cheek. What a flippin bloody ask
Two euros flippin forty? Do they think we're bloody daft?'

It was beautiful flying into Leeds that night
The city lights were shining bright
The sky was clear, the moon was full
And I was happy driving home to Hull

Softy Pofty

We've acquired a dog - a Belgium Malinoir
Which was not a breed I'd ever heard of before
But Oh My God she is gorgeous
And every one of us
Has fallen in love

She's big, she's boisterous and she's beautiful
And wilful. Very wilful.
Sheba is a rescue dog
Who knows her job

Whenever there is a knock at the door - she barks
Whenever she sees a squirrel in the garden - she barks
Whenever she hears another dog bark – she barks
And whenever there is the tiniest noise in the middle of the night –
she barks

And last night
In the middle of the night
She heard something
I was fast asleep and she heard something...
Woof...woof...woof...woof...
Bloody woof

And whilst I go to investigate
She jumps on the bed and nicks my place
'Hey,' I yell, 'You've got a cheek,'
Though I have to admit I admired her technique

'Get down!'
'Get down!'

She looks up and snuggles down
She's the most spoilt dog for miles around
She assumes dead weight and refuses to budge
The only way now is to bribe her with fudge

Then I hear myself go, 'Oood my big, doggie woggie?
Ooood my big softy pofty?
Ooood da most beautiful girl in the whole wide world den?
Ooood a clever girl den?
It's you int it? Yes it is, it's you.
We all love you don't we? Oh yes we do.'

Sheba refutes my attempts to butter her up
There's no way on earth she's going to budge
So I give up
Climb in, give her a shove and nick her fudge

Pigs in Muck

Wouldn't you know it, just our luck
Our new neighbours are common as muck
We can hear them ball and scream and yell and fuck
They call each other 'Duck' and 'Chuck'
Ugh! Darling! Ugh!

They seem to think they're something special
Since crossing the border into well-heeled Hessle
But he lacks that certain fundamental
Class distinction – so essential

Darling, he trims his toe nails out on the patio
He's got a face like a duck-billed platio
How they've got four kids I can't imagino
She's more obliging than I would be - i – o
Ugh! Darling! Ugh!

He parades the garden in his vest and pants
With a can of lager in his hands
He grins at me, he takes a chance
I give him a sign he understands
Ugh! Darling! Ugh!

They ring up their mates – we can them hear of course
Their language, darling, is ever so coarse
'Get your arse out of bed, get yersen ovva 'ere
And don't forget that crate o' beer'

Their mates arrive with the kids in tow
Disturbing the balance and the status quo
Out comes the booze, the burgers and buns
They invite us round to join the fun.

We look at each other in despair
How to refuse and do we dare?
Do we want to be seen 'over there'
With the Lottery Millionaire?
Ugh! Darling! Ugh!

They can't wait to show us their brand spanking new
'Super Duper Barbecue'
And 'Worrabaht this then? This one's legit
'We gorrit off Micky who werks at t'tip'

Two hours later and Meat Loaf's blaring
They're alcohol fuelled and temper's flaring
Every phrase is embroidered with swearing
We let our hair down, we're way past caring
Ooh! Darling! Oooh!

Sharon's copped off wi' John in t'shed
Her old man's g'in 'im a punch in th'ead
And threatened 'im wi' a lump o' lead
And I thought chivalry was dead

Julie's out of it she's smoking a splif
George and Mary have a lover's tiff
Tom gives Henry a Glasgae kiss…
I think I could get into this

All these years I've been missing out
But now I've found what life's about
Smoking, swearing, screaming, shagging
This is what my life's been lacking
Ooh! Darling! Oooh!

We've grown quite fond of Duck and Chuck
They've opened our eyes and livened us up
They're like a breath of fresh air in this neighbourhood
And we're all as happy as pigs in muck

Yes, thanks to our neighbour and his lottery ticket
We've changed our ways, become complicit
And thanks to our friends and Mick at t'tip
We've acquired a barbecue, completely legit.

This'll See Us Out

We'd spent all our lives being responsible
Counting the pennies and being sensible
We'd managed to avoid The Never Never
And contented ourselves with simple pleasure
Card games, monopoly, a walk in the park
A fumble or two in bed after dark

Whoever said, 'Money doesn't make you happy.'
Has never had to scratch for every penny

We used to dream what we'd do if we won The Lottery
And how we would spend all that lovely money
We'd stop entering game shows
And start shopping at Waitrose
Stop buying cheap plonk
And drink what we want

But that of course was a fantasy
Because we don't do The Lottery

So imagine our delight when into our seventies
We received a letter about inheritancies
I screamed at Bill, 'Just look at this! Just look at this!
We can finally start to live a bit.'
We simply couldn't believe our luck
I ran around the house yelling, 'Fuck! Fuck! Fuck!'

Thank you, thank you, Great Aunt Maud
At last we can afford to holiday abroad

The very next day we had a shopping spree
Bought a brand new car and a massive TV
Booked ourselves a holiday or three
Treated ourselves to an afternoon tea
We looked after the family
And donated to charity

And as for friends – we'd never had so many
They were in for a pound and in for a penny

The whole experience was alien to us
In all our lives we'd never argued so much
As we sat either end of our new settee
Watching our Ultra Hi Definition T.V.
Bill moved across and confided in me,
'I don't think we're suited to luxury.

'We're too set in our ways, too long in the tooth
We're way beyond the flush of youth
And let's face it love, there isn't a doubt
That this Hi Def T.V., will see us both out.'
He hadn't planned to say it, it sort of just popped out
It wasn't half a shock to hear it spoken out loud

Then we burst into laughter and agreed it was true
That 'We can live without the money, but not without you.'

They Must Have Come into Money

That family across the road
Wot's their name? Willsden, or summut like that
Anyways, they ant arf bin 'avin' some werk done
I mean to say like, I ain't nosy but…well
Y can't 'elp but notice
I wouldn't mind but they've only bin 'ere two minutes

First they 'ad that kitchen extension
Then a new bathroom went in
Next thing we knew loft were being converted
Nah they've got a conservatory
And a garden room
I mean to say
I say, I mean to say
You don't need both nah d'ya?

They've replaced the drive
There were nowt wrong wi' t'old un
I say, there were nowt wrong wi' it

And if all that weren't enough I saw a summer 'ousey thing arrive today
You mark my werds, that'll be next craze
Summer 'ouses

I wouldn't mind
I say I wouldn't mind but there's only two of 'em
'What are they going to do with all that space?'
Not that I'm jealous or owt
Well, not much anyways

I reckon they must 'av come into money
Lucky beggars

Other stuff

Body Clock

When we arrived in Crete
Those cheeky Greeks
Had altered the clocks!
They'd moved 'em forward
Two hours to fool us

So, while we were there my body clock
Went to pot
I was right out of sync
Sleep patterns, meal times,
All to cock

And it wouldn't be quite so bad
If
When we got back
Our lot
Hadn't gone and altered our clocks
Cheeky sods

One Shot

Life
Is not a dress rehearsal
This is IT
You've got one shot
So don't mess it up

If you get an opportunity
Take it
Grab it with both hands
Because the chances are
It won't come knocking again

You can't go back and change what you've done
Or not done
Or wish you'd done

Treat people kindly
Show respect
But don't take any shit
Because this is your life

You've got one shot
Make it count

Flash

You can keep your posh Parkers and Mont Blancs
Your Schaeffers, Watermans and Duponts
Your Caran d'Ache
Your Diplomat
They're too flash for me

I can't write with a fountain pen
I doubt I'll ever use one again
All those splots and splodges
Pads of blotters
They're not for me

The Fisher Space Pen was a possibility
A friend of a friend gave one to me
A pen renown
For writing upside down
But it wasn't for me

The Russians looked askance at the Space Pen
And quickly decided it wasn't for them
Though they deemed writing in space to be surely essential
They kept it simple and took a pencil
I admired their ability
To think laterally
Flash stuff wasn't for them

I prefer a bic, I find them uniquely
Straight forward and easy
Their grip enables me to write quite neatly
There's no la di dah
No blah di blah
A bic is…well…they are what they are

Cheap, unpretentious,
And absolutely flippin' stupendous

What Might My Mother Say?

I can only imagine what my mother might say
If she could see the way we live today
One thing I'm certain she'd be sure to ask
Would be, 'Why does no-one carry any cash?'
And, 'Whatever happened to the threepenny bits
The tanners, half crowns and bobs?
There was nothing wrong with shillings and pence
This decimal lark just doesn't make sense

And

I don't understand this 'banking on line'
Or how goods get delivered in double quick time
Why wherever you shop you're asked for a card
For the pounds and pence there's little regard

And

You queue up at the Supermarket to serve yourself
Put your goods on a till which talks to itself
Pack all your shopping without any help
It can't be good for your mental health

And

Don't get me going about politics
I could scream my head off at those lunatics
And the silly sods who voted them in
The world's gone mad, my head's in a spin

And

What's all this about climate change?
I admit at first, I thought it sounded strange
But sad to say it all adds up
We're governed by greed and the world's corrupt'

Then

She concluded with words so wise
'Beware of those with self-serving lies
Stay true to yourself and question who's right
Shout out loud in the dark of the night
Be brave, stay strong and fight, fight, fight
And always remember to write, write, write
Because words are important, you have to try, try, try
Or I fear the world will fry, fry, fry.'

Supermarket Shopping

(A Rant)

I drive to the Supermarket
Park the Car
Take the bags from the car
Collect a trolley
Spend a good half hour finding the stuff I need
Put it in my trolley

Spend more time picking up stuff I didn't know I needed but it
seems like a good idea right now
I pick up even more stuff that I definitely don't need but I think I'll
get it anyway
Because 'It'll make a change'
And it's that sort of a day

Satisfied with myself
I head towards the tills

Problem

There are long queues at the 'proper' tills
I.e. the ones with actual people operating them

Everyone in the queue seems to have trolleys loaded with stuff
they need
Stuff they don't need
Stuff they bought because they thought it looked 'nice for a change.'
Because it's that sort of a day

I join the shortest queue

Bad choice

There is a problem with an item which has no bar code
There is a problem with a bust bag of sugar
There is a problem when the customer clocks a squashed orange in
the bag of oranges
There is a problem getting a supervisor to the till
There is a problem with the queue getting fed up of waiting

I decide to be brave
For the first time I decide I'll use the self-service tills
You know where you have to remove all your items from your trolley
And put it on the conveyor belt
Then scan the items one by one through the till
Put them in the bag in the bagging area
Then put them all back in the trolley
Load them into the car
And take them home

It goes swimmingly for about four items
I congratulate myself
'Why was I so worried? Ha ha this is easy.'

The till has stopped
A message comes up on the screen
'Supervisor required'
I'm shocked, 'Why? What have I done wrong?'
I'm sweating and a bag of nerves
'Why did I decide to do this?'

The supervisor arrives
She's pleasant. Helpful.
She taps a few numbers in the till
And we're off again

I gain a bit of confidence
Put more stuff through
It's going well
I'm on a roll now
Finding those bar codes is a piece of cake
I'm kicking ass

Until
The till talks to me
This is new to me.
And it's quite loud
No subtlety
It says,
'There is a surprising item in the bagging area'

I get quite excited
What is the surprising item?
Have I won a prize for the most efficient self-service till user today?

No
It would appear not

I'm disappointed

The supervisor comes across
Taps in a few more numbers
Moves the bags in the bagging area
Explains the system

I feel embarrassed
And stupid
It feels like everyone is looking at me
Tutting and tapping their fingers
I try to ignore them
I plod on

Surely I can't be the only one to struggle?
That supervisor has her work cut out
Running between tills
Helping people like me who can't seem to get it right
She'll never get fat

It takes me ages but eventually I manage it
I've put everything through the till and bagged it all up
Result!

I confidently pay with my credit card, collect the receipt
I load all the bags into the trolley
And head towards the car

I check my watch
It's taken me a good twenty minutes to negotiate my way around
that self-service till
It would have been much quicker to queue and let a 'proper' person
serve me
It's a bloody con

Anyway, onwards and homewards
I unload the shopping from the trolley into the car
I drive home
It takes four trips from the house to the car and back again to
unload the bags into the house
I put the kettle on
I put the shopping away

I think, 'I'll treat myself to one of those chocolate biscuits I bought
but didn't need'
'I deserve it'

But then, damn it, guess what?
I've forgotten the tea bags
And the bread
And the milk
And the spuds

I'll have to go back
Or send Bill
I think I'll send Bill
He should try his hand at this
He should know how stressful it is

He goes off looking cocky
I think, 'He'll learn.'

He returns home within half an hour
Pleased as punch with himself

He's used those 'new self-service tills'
No problem!
Easy!

AAAARRRRRGGGGGHHHH!

I hide the biscuits I bought but didn't need.
There's only one left and it's mine.

Over-Cooked

TV programmes like Master Chef,
And The Great British Bake Off
Scare people off
Who can't cook
Who don't know how to cook
Who've never been taught to cook

Saturday Kitchen doesn't inspire them
To 'have a go at that in my kitchen'
It leaves them feeling clueless
And useless

Flashing their knives with lightning speed
The TV chefs and celebrities
Blithely advise on what goes with what
Whilst assuring us that, 'It doesn't cost a lot.'

They're oblivious that your average Joe
Simply doesn't want to know
About cous cous, quinoa and fancy rices
He takes a look and clocks up the prices
And thinks, 'Well, that's all very well but it's easier
And cheaper
To feed my family on a takeaway pizza'

Whilst the smug judges (the pretentious gits)
Assert an anxious competitor's dish is
'A little over cooked'
'A little undercooked'
Or, with a superior air claim it is, 'For you, darling, ever so slightly
over-ambitious'
Before condescendingly admitting, 'Your sauce though, darhhling,
is truly delicious.'

They refuse to acknowledge that the family budget
Is frequently based on chicken nuggets
They're blissfully unaware that your average Joe
Is keen to learn and just needs to know
The basics
Like how to chop and stir and mix
Whip up a batter, and fry a steak
Then maybe one day, he'll bake a cake

These programmes have undermined Joe's confidence
It's destroyed the little faith he had in himself
Downhearted he reaches for the phone and orders a Margarita
Pizza
Whilst he waits feeling angry and bitter
He checks his face book account and twitter
He clicks onto YouTube and types in 'Food'
He discovers exciting facts about the Oxo Cube

Inspired he fries up mushrooms and tomatoes
He smiles and says, 'That'll do for starters
'Today a pizza topping, tomorrow the world
Roasts and pickles and lemon curd
Casseroles, cakes and buns and quiches
Oriental dishes from Vietnameases

Nowadays there's no stopping Joe
He's hosts lavish parties, he makes his own dough
And it's all thanks to YouTube, that fount of all knowledge
And no thanks whatsoever to that puffed up Greg Wallace

Persist

What if there were no crime or war?
What if there were no space to explore?
What if Bernstein hadn't composed that score?
Wouldn't life become an awful bore?

What if there were no lies or greed?
What if everyone always agreed?
What would happen if our kids didn't succeed?
Would it mean as parents we'd under achieved?

What if there were no disease or famine?
What if there were no poetry slammin'?
What if musicians stopped their jammin'?
What if Heinz stopped their baked bean cannin'?

What if in life there were no 'what ifs?'
No 'even thoughs', amongst the mix
If rage or sadness didn't exist
Would the poets still persist?
Persist? Persist? Persist t...t...t...t?

Tiddly Dum

Some people today don't know they're born
Tiddly dum
They have far too much and that's their norm
Tiddly dum, tiddly dum, tiddly dum dum dum

But some are on the streets and they can't keep warm
Tiddly dum
A cardboard box their uniform
Tiddly dum, tiddly dum, tiddly dum dum dum

They're under nourished, pale and drawn
Tiddly dum
They're being exploited and used for porn
Tiddly dum, tiddly dum, tiddly dum dum dum

We're living in a world where greed is the norm
Tiddly dum
Where values are distorted, warped and torn
Tiddly dum, tiddly dum, tiddly dum dum dum

I yearn for a future where honesty's the norm
Where the kids on the street aren't used for porn
Where the down and outs are helped to perform
And where low life scammers are shot at dawn/eventually reform
Tiddly dum, tiddly dum, tiddly dum dum dum

Tiddly dum, tiddly dum, tiddly dum dum dum

You can't go wrong

'Ooooh!' he said, 'You can't go wrong,
Just take the first right, the second left, carry on right up to the top,
There's a bit of a bend in the road and you'll go past the pub
Now then, what's it called? Is it The Red Lion, or the Black Horse?
I say, Iris, what's the pub called at the top there, you know the one,
Just past the bend?'

Iris, always one to lend a hand, leans in, asks, 'Where do you want
to be, love?'
'The Remembrance Hall, Main Road,'
'Ooooh!' Iris exclaims, 'You can't go wrong, just go straight to the
top here and take a left,
Then across the cross roads and it's somewhere on your right.
That's right isn't it Jeff?'
Exasperated Jeff shouts, 'No, that's the Church Hall, he wants the
Remembrance Hall,'

'Oooh, sorry love, oh, right, The Remembrance Hall,
'That would be the one with the double doors
'Ooooh, that's easy, you can't go wrong,
'First right, second left, up to the top, round the bend,
'Past the pub. Now then, what's it called? Jeff, what's that pub called?
'Is it The Duke or The Jolly Roger?'

I give in.
I climb back into my car and leave them arguing about the name of
the pub.
They don't even see me leave   ·
I take the first left and follow the signs.
The signs peter out
And I do manage to go wrong.

I do what I should have done in the first place and turn on the Sat Nav

Friday Night Drama

Oh great! Here we go again, something else to look forward to
on the telly
Another over the top, hyped up, Friday night Drama
Another Drama I won't understand
Another Drama with so many twists and turns I doubt even the
writer knows who dunnit

Another 6 weeks of struggling with the plot
Another 6 weeks wondering who's lying and who's not
Another 6 weeks of critics critiquing
Another 6 weeks being told it's intriguing

Another 6 weeks of actors mumbling their lines
Another 6 weeks wondering who done the crime
Or what it is or where it's set
Or who it is that's supposed to be dead?

Surely I can't be the only one
Who cannot grasp what's going on
Why I'm no further forward than when it begun
But I'm thinking that maybe the killer's her son?

We're into week five and the guy from week one
Has turned up on her doorstep and he's carrying a gun
I didn't expect that, I'm really shocked
Why didn't the silly cow keep her door locked?

In these dramas it's always the same
Someone does something completely insane
The intention is to increase the tension
Drive us off course and divert our attention
It's the writer's fault, I'll swear it's deliberate
It's a whisker short of damned inconsiderate

Week 6 arrives and it's the big reveal
I knew that tow rag would be the one to squeal
I said from week one it was sure to be him
He had the look of a killer and his name was ...Jim

What a rubbish ending and they've left the door open
For addicts like me who're hooked on emotion
I hope it's not long before they screen another
Friday night drama of undercover

87

Shackled

There was no escape
No way out
No choice
At least, that's how it felt

The kids needed her
She was pregnant again
He'd planned that
Not her

He reckoned
Another bun in the oven would keep her there
Shackled
For a few more years
Until some other innocent, inexperienced, impressionable
young woman came along
And fell for his garbage

Some other vulnerable, desperate, no family to speak
of young woman
Isolated and starved of affection
In need of love
Who for a few short weeks would believe him to be the man
of her dreams
Before discovering
He was the man of her nightmares

An uneducated, cruel, controlling creep
Who laughed in her face
Who scorned her tears
Beat her and told her she was only good for one thing

He'd apologise the next day
'I promise I won't do it again,' he'd weep
'It's the beer talking
'You know I love you.'

That was Nev's pattern.
That was how he worked
That was his system
And women fell for it
Again and again

He left a trail of unplanned kids in his wake
Broken women
And savagely, infuriated friends
Including Marcus
Who showed up very early one morning
And beat the shit out of him

Moon Time

I've heard of Spring Time
Summer Time
Autumn Time
And Winter Time

I've heard of Start Time
Last Time
Getting ahead of Time
And being lost in Time

And I recently learned of Moon Time

'They'
I.e. the powers that be
Are going to create a New Time
And call it 'Moon Time'
Because for what it's worth
Time runs slower there than it does on earth
A whole one second slower
Every 50 years

Wow!

Apparently, time for the astronauts must be absolutely accurate
Otherwise, it causes chaos
With their experiments and departures
I have to admit
It stretches my imagination a bit
Especially when I think of the 63 bus
That is, of course, when it bothers to turn up

Moon Mad Millionaires

I wonder if Moon Time would be important to the millionaires
Who have time on their hands and money to spare?
Will those Moon Mad Tourists
With more money than sense
Be queueing up soon
To visit The Moon?

I guess they would boast and brag to their friends
About how much it cost and the money they'd spent
The amazing food and accommodation
The views of earth from their exotic location
Claim the experience was 'second to none'
And that zero gravity was 'such fun'

But Moon travel is not for me
I mean, why go to The Moon when there's bugger all to see?
An alien landscape with no infra structure
No cinemas, theatres, history or culture
No people, no buildings, no scenery
No rivers, no mountains, no greenery

Frankly I'd rather go to Brid
It's cheaper than the moon by a fair few quid
I can walk on the front with the Kiss-Me-Quicks
Dodge the gulls trying to nick me chips
Indulge in an ice cream with a flake and bits
Admire the puffins on Bempton Cliffs

Sometimes it's nice to reminisce
About the times we had when we were kids
Buckets and spades and a packet of crisps
Who needs The Moon when we've got all this?

Little Things

It's not the big gestures
It's the little ones

Running the bath
Putting a hot water bottle in the bed
Holding the door open
Saying you look nice
Noticing when you've had your hair done
Or when you're upset

Listening
Hearing
Caring

Kindness
Gentleness

Honesty
Generosity

Being there

Sticking up for you even when you've got it wrong

Having a laugh
Reminiscing
Being together with no need for words
Holding your hand

It's the little things

Day by day

The Dress

There's a dress in my wardrobe that won't go away
It's been there for years and it's determined to stay
I bought it for a wedding – a right posh do
I haven't worn it since and it looks like new

It's old fashioned now but somehow
I don't have the heart to throw it out
Because one day I might need it again
Should I feel the need to look fabulous again

The couple who married now have children
They've moved abroad - moved on
Progressed
Done well

Meanwhile, my dress still hangs
Forlornly, hopefully
Waiting for a 'do'

The thing is if I were to wear it now I would feel as though
I were dressed for a wedding
Like I should be going to a wedding
Then today I thought – I could wear that dress again if
I wore it with different shoes.
Because they make a difference don't they – shoes?

Yes. Shoes are the answer …or possibly boots…sandals… trainers??
No. No. It has to be shoes.
Now then what colour shall I go for and what style shall I choose?

Once a Year

It's Spring, it's 4.00 a.m.
And the dawn chorus is starting up again
It's deafening

The owls have gone to bed
But the blackbird is up
As ever the early bird

It's summer
Long, hot, sticky days
Pot plants gasping for a drink

Next doors are outside having a row
Their kids are inside on their computers oblivious
The dog pants, looking from one to the other, he just wants a quiet life

It's Autumn, it's beautiful
It's windy
And it's raining leaves

The nights are drawing in
It's cooler
Time for Strictly

It's Winter
Long, cold, dark nights
Hugging hot water bottles

Brazenly Christmas arrives
Shouting at us to be happy
Demanding we be sociable

Exhausted we smile as expected
We give presents we can't afford
And receive the same
'Oh, you shouldn't have.'
'I know. But I thought, well you know…
It's only once a year.'

It's a Con

Many moons ago a business man made a smart decision
To resolve his cash flow problem he'd invent a new religion
His mission was to rule the world, he was ruthless, he was cruel
He set up shop and got to work and soon was on a roll

His strategy was cunning, his attitude cut-throat
He played on people's feelings and their desperate need of hope
He preyed upon the vulnerable, the old, the weak, the sick
His psychopathic tendencies helped him know what made them tick

He understood the power of fear, he understood the mind
He portrayed himself as caring, gentle, warm and kind
He was very charismatic as he preached his pack of lies
And with his home-made gospel the people were inclined
To believe they'd found a saviour, someone honest, someone true
Who would lead them to salvation – for their hard-earned pound or two

They opened up their hearts to him and furthermore their purses
They simply didn't understand there would be no reimburses
They entrusted him with secrets, their failings from the past
He made a note of their confessions and soon the die was cast
He used the information to corrupt and bribe and cheat
This man they thought their hero was a master of deceit

He robbed them of their savings and their reputations too
Too late they realised he was a con man through and through
Shocked they checked their bank accounts
Outraged they did announce
To the media, to one and all,
'We've been bloody 'ad!'

'By that dirty, devious, cheating sod, that rotten, little squirt
Give me half an hour with him and I'll kick him where it hurts
I said I didn't like him, I always said he was a crook
But you refused to listen and you said I was mistook
And now he's off with our hard-earned cash
Cruising the Med and out on the lash
Masquerading as a Man of God
If I could I'd have him shot'

And every single one of them has now renounced religion
They offer their views to anyone who has a mind to listen
'Religion controls the working man
And lines the pockets of the bloody scum
The fact is love, when you're gone, you're gone
There is no God to rely upon
Salvation's nowt but a bloody con.'